SEP   2001   811.54 KNOTT
Knott, Bill, 1940
The quicken tree.

P9-AGM-307

BOA
EDITIONS
LIMITED

WITHDRAWN

The Quicken Tree

Poems by Bill Knott

BOA Editions, Ltd.   ❧   Brockport, NY   ❧   1995

ALAMEDA FREE LIBRARY
2200-A CENTRAL AVENUE
ALAMEDA, CA 94501

Copyright © 1995 by Bill Knott
All rights reserved
Manufactured in the United States of America

LC #: 95–79361
ISBN: 1–880238–24–1 cloth
ISBN: 1–880238–25–X paper

First Edition
95 96 97 98   7 6 5 4 3 2 1

The publication of books by BOA Editions, Ltd.,
a not-for-profit corporation under section 501 (c) (3)
of the United States Internal Revenue Code,
is made possible with the assistance of grants from
the Literature Program of the New York State Council on the Arts
and the Literature Program of the National Endowment for the Arts,
as well as from the Lannan Foundation,
the Rochester Area Foundation, the County of Monroe, NY,
and contributions by individual supporters.

Cover Design: Daphne Poulin-Stofer
Art: Detail from "Song" by DeLoss McGraw
Typesetting: Richard Foerster
Manufacturing: McNaughton & Gunn, Lithographers
BOA Logo: Mirko

BOA Editions, Ltd.
A. Poulin, Jr., President
92 Park Avenue
Brockport, NY 14420

ALAMEDA FREE LIBRARY
2264 CENTRAL AVENUE
ALAMEDA, CA 94501

To Rochelle Nameroff with love

*—And with thanks for the kindness of many,
foremost of whom are Thomas Lux and Mary Karr
and DeWitt Henry*

CONTENTS

Part One

Part Two

Part Three

Part One

SYMMETRY

How mirrored this merging, how lover/loved—
How love aligns us and aims to make our skins
Correspond, each of your pores barrel-grooved
With one of mine, clone-gunned: then void opens
Onto void, grid-ideal, union, see, it joins!
First of course the skins have to be removed.

STRESS THERAPY

Time, time, time, time, the clock
vaccinates us,
and then even that lacks
prophylaxis.

Ticktock-pockmarked, stricken
by such strokes, we
get sick of prescriptions
which work solely

on the body.
Systole diastole—
It is by its very

intermittency
that the heart knows
itself to be an I.

VISION OF THE GODDESS IN A CITY SUMMER

to Carolyn Kizer

And yet what if the sweat that breaks
Even from Her feet as they pass
Can never rain these pavements back
To a mud- a milk-cud grass

Time that diamond instant dew dulls
Is it quicker than them quote
That strode presence those fading puddles
Not in this goadless heat

Oh mirage oh haze of hydrants
Go Isis-proud across crosswalks
Leave brief seas without a halt

Till all my doubts dissolve at once
And down I'll follow cowed to lick
Your soleprints for my salt

THE SEVEN LAST WORDS
OF SOFIA GUBAIDULINA

Intestinal as raisins on a keyboard
I struggled through life. The setting sun
left a few earths in the ground so I could walk.

It qualmed me just knowing that, to accomplish my color,
the chameleon must die. How chastely I
watched a suit-of-armor chew its fingernails.

Oh voice scathed in cloud; ankles' adieu.
On the lips—that species of slither—is where
I took part.

Now I pestle my face with opaque pins. You
stigmata that summarize my signature, go,
hinges down whom antiquity has vomited sequence—

but which letter misnomers my name? I come
from neitherstood, nuance of none. I tried
to obey the caption under my portrait/my provenance.

Cere me in cerberus-lily; in theme-mother extracts;
while the loaves and fish rich, the furs and lush rich,
fill their skin with pores and then wonder what's missing . . .

Like a candle through a keyhole
shoved, burning toward knownwheres—
Always the days unstay me.

I need to have admired more those symmetries which preach
each seed is buried beneath a flower,
each weed above a wound.

Now the thorns be praised/now the thrall that somehow
time has restored en masse my dwelling,
my resting place. I hope my pillow's hungry for headaches!

Note:
Inspired by Gubaidulina's partita, *The Seven Last Words* (1982).

FROZEN

to RN

Oh I know it must feel
Measureful

To be the river—
Source of that force

Each field each flower
Each fountain seeks—

And then of course
I have to shiver

Remembering how—
How few of us ever

Make it down
These mountain peaks.

EMIGRATIONS

for Heather McHugh

Shouldn't there be a word that sounds like an
extraterrestrial clearing his throat
of human phrases, their roughness roseate,
plush thorns that tart each normal timbre—
And when that word's punctuated by two ears,
can it be said to not hold all our meanings?

Vocal as those envelopes one discovers
tell-traces of tongue-blood on the flap of
(licked too reckless—mistake it for love),
we fail to seal shut the heart, to kissproof
its distant alien stains: kept vigilant over
that bouquet of papercuts, I remember

a cloud installed with thumbtacks scouting
across planet, pinning down oceans, denoting
islands, deserts. Borders, poured from the sky—
We felt safe on such worlds, behind guards,
armies braced to rebuff incursor postcards.
Death rose to greet us with a flower in its eye.

*

But count the kisses, Catullus wrote, meaning
to waste your time first multiply your tongue.
Oh make that prime mistake again; repeat
what the explorers of sea-roared corridors
promise each conch that coils them, desperate
to remain unsounded, sole. All such figures

are promiscuous: love is repetition
and layer/layer lovers disrobe; overlapping
matteshots which hatch-depict what deepest down
most elusive nudity. Our stripped-off skin hurts
to acknowledge the body is the blankest map
onto which earth will eventually start

to imprint itself dirtgrain by dirtgrain,
mud by mire it will come to cover us entire
with minutiae of the utter matter
ground around us until we are its textual
affirmation, and therefore a refutation
of what? The self—but if its loss is a sexual

discovery, the poet has entered hell
demanding to plumb whomever these charts
misquote. À la Cocteau's torturous *Orphée*,
she guides herself through fog-stellar hallways;
every step begs to be reversed. Their cry
is always the same: what exquisite urge

to tame all welcome-mats has portaged us
averted, shielding our gaze from its suffice,
to this place! Waving an exit visa stamped
with each other's lips, the lovers have sailed
beyond i.d. But the ship sinks, no-one can build
enough lighthouses to surround that swamp—

*

Orpheus croaks, the frog in his larynx jokes,
each time Euridice crumples backwards, implodes
from sight: he is what she breaks—his grid, his husk.
When the sperm disembowels my orgasm, he asks,
what self-restraint it shows to commit suicide
in front of a mirror, knowing beauty is

personalized by paralysis . . . then, if the wound
learns to probe for its own kind, flesh will never
unvoice that loss, harvest that scar. By harping on
her name he hopes to gloss, to refine this epitaph.
Meanwhile the eternal tatter of her smile flares
fainter, firefly trying to land down a mineshaft.

Fact: the frog can't see the fly if the fly sits—
it is literally its flight obscenes the eyes
whereupon the long tongue zaps out, severs and appetites.
With this in mind, perhaps the truest desire is
blind, concealed, a phantom wandering the deep net
of optic intersections, of pang-swerved nerves—

lost, one of its possible fates might be starve.
The poet traverses this labyrinth—the maze carves
emaciations from her face. Her way is gropes
which somehow render aim that inner landscape
our window (at night the white moth's easel) drapes,
that site razed by home. But could she place her poem

if it moved her mouth with mine so they became
one, one mouth which then looked for another
mouth to kiss. It first appears there are only
two bodies here—the one you are, and the one
you desire to unite with. But then, beyond
the mingle of that longed-for synthesis, we

may hunger for more antitheses, further
incarnations, until (exponentially)
our body orbits what rapt apogee, that pure
theory. I believe it. And thus to make them whole
your lips must be divided by these words. She
who utters such catharsis/communion will

have to seed or sate whatever wing-hung thing
we nurse in our throatpit. Gordian gorge:
just ingest each knot and trust—trust your intestines
will undo it? Orpheus or Herpheus, the poet
cannot reduce the roughage verbiage her diet
imposes on us since it is our emptiness, purged.

*

*We who journey towards tomorrow rather than
today walk behind a door which our arms are tired
of holding held out in front of us, the wrists ache
from its weight—although our knuckles come to admire
the knob—merely on the stray-or-none chance the one
who bears our key may be heading yesterday's way.*

(PLEA, HOPELESS, SUB VOCE)

Murderous the gist
of their paws condemns
us all to die of applause:
in this circus minimus
even Coriolanus must
nurse and gnaw and showcase
his scars when the next
closeup comes.

                  (—But not my poems!)

ENVY-EROT-ETCET

Sexshorn in a fanfare museum, where
my kisses' strings crisscross Picasso's mattress—
I gropejob its lumps, those dents creases
scored by his endless corps of mistresses,

how cogently they queued up to lie there;
just one of the icons the fetishes
I mount in myself to make myself more jealous:
look, Anaïs Nin's douche wig, it's here

too, in this exhibit. As if spitballs
when they hit split/became origami—
But the transformation can't be that

instant-childlike, can it? I wring it
all over my lips my love my lust for
those poets whose pics appear in *APR*.

AT MY GRANDCLONE'S GRAVE

You said that hair was merely the head out of focus
and thus for a man, for me, growing old and bald must
mean entering the picture is leaving it. And yet, here,
when the cemetery grass paints my toenails with smoke I

need you to refute me more the ground I walk on,
not cloud. That uncarpeted core of space is where
there's too much perch to pose for polaroid-deviled scans—
they sun us toward life's Project Face, as if death

is young enough to get i.d. Gee it de-I.Q.'s me
to hear you say that skimming through nulls and skies negatives
the event to wait for a burial that involves

just ourself: see these forehead plod lines, the skull the flesh
which wings washed from me at birth have daubed listless
verdure over, the gaze ending so firmly in lax?

ANOTHER HOLE FOR W.R. RODGERS

Speak like a singularity, a lack
residing deep inside every lock, just
past the point keys can jab: against all thrusts
make safe-ensure your door's core is held back,

for reckless access to this pure center
quarks more quintessence than taking exits
from those pried voids whose secret quickly sates:
ubiquitous if Space presses Enter.

Which inadmissible sill still calls us
with imagine: our skeleton keeping
each such portal neither open nor shut,

unhoused of that exclusive airborne dust
we breathe, though there must be something
it accumulates, accommodates: what?

IN MEMORIAM

What the Year Says:
  I am a bud.
  I am a blossom.
  I am a leaf.
  I am a branch.

What the Year Doesn't Say:
  I'm burgeoning.
  I'm ripe.
  I'm falling.
  I'm bare.

What John Logan Said to Me in the Year 1960:
  Show, don't tell.

TO THE EMBLEMATIC HOURGLASS
OF MY FATHER'S SKULL

The night that dies in me each day is yours:
Hour whose way I stare, yearning to terra
Firma my eye. There. Where a single hair
Would be a theater curtain I could cling

Behind, dreading my cue, aching to hear
What co-hurrah. More, more of leaves that fall
Consummate capsules, having annaled all
Their veins said! Printout *printemps*. And yet

(Altars our blood writes a blurb for god on)
Can one ever envy enough his skeleton's
Celebrity. Can any epitaph

Be adequate repartee for your laugh.
Days lived by me each night say less than it.
While sleep in ounces weighs me wanting.

FUTURISM

Hours in the wristwatch,
moments in the wrist—who's counting?

Minutehands
choked in a fist, we sin

and tell the day to die. Still,
will a clock ever be real

to us until time ends; similarly,
can a cemetery

truly exist
before

we are immortal—
only once past

their utility
may these entities be perceived

as they are innate, in
essence. We would see them then

for the first time
as them

and not as the medium
we made of them—

To see each thing beyond its use is
to see ourselves past hope

in an earliest end perhaps
where, re Gautier, everything

useful is ugly. Everyday
a big robot will come

and wind us up
until we scream—

But listen to your pulse:
its beat, its beauty

is eternity's whim:
bim boom bim

Note:
Lines 24-25: "Only that which cannot serve a purpose may be considered truly
beautiful. Everything that is useful is ugly, for usefulness expresses human
needs, and they are base and debilitating."—from Théophile Gautier's preface
to *Mademoiselle de Maupin*.

Part Two

MENAGERIE OF THE AEDILES

Now what thought is thrashing from this brain to be
unleashed by a brow-to-brow collision with
a unicorn? Or could it go released through
other throes I wonder. For if I were gored

there, mightn't I, like, die? When *Terminator* zaps
a hole in someone's forehead they don't write
a poem response, they drop and he steps on them
crunch, french, act, your soundtrack may vary.

The plan was to get scalpels taped to the Creature
From The Fuck's huge flipper-tentacles and
then lie down hoping that perhaps those wild wave ways

surgically correct my defect my gender—
penis revealed as gap in consciousness—
Though I know none of you beasts loves me that much.

BREATH/LOST

At dawn I see across the way the treetops
seem to crouch, unlit yet, waiting for sun
to turn them tall again. I yawn, I stretch—
the day's first stretch, when the body, after

lying scrunched up all night, reconnects with
its cardinal quadrants, the four points that
encompass us: each limb jars the edge of,
marks out and wakes the corners of our cage.

Oh window! I am complete with this caught breath,
this space suffice on which even paper
airplanes must float, updraft that elevates

eyes to ritual heights, those clouds morning
throws passersbird down through to gaud the good
before I forget that it alone is my nest.

My diaries may be jammed to the Dec.s
with the return dates of comets,
but monitors track the orbits
I tunnel from. Every door connects

for this omen-minotaur: zoom-in
a queen running down a Paul Klee
walkways maze, filmstar footprints I
set out to portray on my skin.

Framed by the errand dole of dream,
REM thumbs my nerves like gloves
molding a voodoo doll museum,
its corridors recurrent as waves

pacing their birthplace backwards—
exit whose wax I blaze skies towards.

GRANT PROPOSAL (Category: Performance Arts)

I want to go out each day at noon and stand
On top of our Capitol's highest highrise,
Where aircurrents stack, where storms reassemble,
Where the crossroads of sky are swept by radar,

Up there, buffeted, stand, cupping in my hands
A gleam of gold-dust, a handful of gold-dust
Doled out to me each day by our State, by you
The modest mandarins of its Arts Council,

Trustees all, you whose grace I must stand for there
And being thus empowered begin to pour
The gold-dust back and forth, pour it in sifts from

Hand to hand until the wind has left my palms
Bare, please note that length of project will vary
Daily, at noon, and not one grain remains.

Notes:
Line 2: Capitol with an 'o'—meaning "the citadel of government" (OED), its cloistered towers, atop the tallest of which the applicant desires to venture.
Line 6: maybe "gleam" should be "flash"? I associate the former with earth, the latter, sky. "In the things that arise [structures or buildings of any sort], earth is present as the sheltering agent," Heidegger swears in 'The Origin of the Work of Art.' "Berg" (castle/citadel) is etymologically linked to "bury": what bears Fort Knox Knott if not that?
Hendecasyllabics, with a variant last line.

THE HUNGER

If a path to the Gingerbread House
could be established by breaking crumbs
off its edifice and sprinkling them
so as to find what lies behind us

across the featureless fairytale
void of childhood: yet how very quick
that trick wears out when the story's track
takes hold, takes toll, a far-older trail

prevails, we're forced to give up this lost
cause; and the fact is that every last
morsel was gone long before the you

or I might totter our way back here
to try to dissuade all these other
Hansel-Gretels hollering in queue.

THE SONNET IN *ix*

The nube, the nude, the not—you know: the Nix—
Her Septet of orifices? (males have six):—
Was it massed by Master Malyoume for the fix
The fucks. Rape-sleeve: she, some defunc'-off, kicks

The mirror while centaurs click centerfold pics
Of her fingernails—each closeup mimics
The anguish with which our pallored poet sics
Midnights on. Encore encore, you sexniks,

Steph calls, tiptoeing away toward his sonics
Lab, 'The Sign in X.' A thousand-quicksand thicks
His step. He's pitbogged by all the nitpicks

Critics have glitched his path with, those pricks!
Don't they know that stars—stars can't hold shit wicks
To his candle?! (That bitch, that *Nix: he* sucks it: "I-icks!")

Notes:
Failed translation of Stéphane Mallarmé's 'Sonnet en yx.' Line 14: "I-icks!"
(both i's are short, as in "kiss") is an onomatopoeticism that accompanies the
expectoration and or taste of the candle's cum. Sort of the sound you make
when you use your teeth to scrape it off your tongue ostentatiously. But why
did I end the poem this way? Was I influenced by the Master's regret, expressed
in his essay *Crise de Vers*, that words lack an embodied, material, tonal
consonance with their meanings: "Quelle déception" (he writes), how per-
verse, that the "timbres" of the word "jour" should be dark, while those of
"nuit" are "clair." And yet, he concludes, without such "défaut des langues,"
poetry itself would not exist. Assuming he's right, then onomatopoeia are
defective because they're not defective. In Japanese, kireji—"cutting-words,
used to separate or set off statements"—are onomatopoeic, and "have the
meaning that lies in themselves as sounds." But as Hiroaki Sato notes (in his
book, *One Hundred Frogs*, from which I've taken these quotes): "Bashō
himself simply said, 'Every sound unit is a kireji.'" In any case, the faults and
falls and false of my trans. should be clair to all.

EPIGRAM *(Plus ça change . . .)*

When young,
I was attracted to what they call
Older women.

Older now,
I am attracted to what they call
Old women.

CHRISTMAS AT THE ORPHANAGE

But if they'd give us toys and twice the stuff
most parents splurge on the average kid,
orphans, I submit, need more than enough;
in fact, stacks wrapped with our names nearly hid
the tree: these sparkling allotments yearly
guaranteed a lack of—what?—family?—

I knew exactly what it was I missed
as we were lined up number rank and file:
to share my pals' tearing open their piles
meant sealing the self, the child that wanted
to scream at all *You stole those gifts from me;*
whose birthday is worth such words? The wish-lists
they'd made us write out in May lay granted
against starred branches. I said I'm sorry.

2 FUTILISTS

Even if the mountain I climbed
Proved to be merely a duncecap
It was only on gaining its peak
That that knowledge reached me.

*

Is there a single inch—
one square millimeter
on the face of our planet
which some animal
human or otherwise
has not shit on?

Is there anywhere even
a pore's-worth of ground—
earth that has never
(not once in its eons)
been covered by what
golgotha of dung?

If such a place exists,
I want to go there
and stand there
at that site
in that spot, truly
and purely for an instant.

7 $^1/_2$ POEMS TO, FOR, AND ABOUT RN

1. Substitute

If you have licked the whiteout off this poem,
then it exists: go on, strip it, stroke its wordwad.

Down its page-plunge, distribute our briefhood;
my flesh is blonde, my bones must be brunette.

Have I loved enough my planet's comet habits?
Look, how my blushes stain lambs. Oh shame-thumbed,

obelisk of hailstones, text rhymes with innermost:
to regain that clarity whereby it kills,

the vial of poison must be shaken, or jacked off—
I have failed to decentralize my navel.

Now my balding hairs are wove to make your hats;
my toenail clippings, glued, fused, used for your shoe-soles;

notice the metonymy. I myself am composed
of everything you excrete bleed sweat etcet.

2. What Missing Her Is Like

It's like ripping your fingernails off
drying them out
then carefully placing each nail
back on its particular tip
just resting it there

no glue or anything
then trying to juggle them all in place
so entirely normally that
the people you're with
never even suspect

(I omit
the blood scabs scars part of it)

3.   Dyed

I deny every emergence of the night
From your hair, crevice that heavies me
Though I waver as water- or age-stained pages;
Do hushpoints accompany such cries?

Your skeleton/scrupulous abacus where
Flesh's inconsistent total of hope,
Despair, recurs, keeps score, where
Skin has no right to interrupt my pores.

Depictured (which in the distance pales) who
—Oh bright, pagoda-forgotten landscape!
Where moths spared myths of flame come, go.
Near where the nevers flow into the no.

4.   Buried

Sometimes I think she believes in
the Catastrophe Theory—
that her falling into and then
out of love with me was surely

based on the trend of Nemesis
(that changeling twin of our sun):
each lovefall seemed as sudden, as
doomed-to-be as the extinction

of what Saurian habitat.
Whole species annihilated—
some, I haven't uncovered yet.
But all, I better believe it, dead.

(They'll clone that dino DNA—
can love be revived that way?)

5. Long Distance Affair

The saliva gathered daily
in telephones across the world
from lovers yelling at each other
is an ocean with no bottom.

But say you pried apart those phones
you'd find that all that wild white tide
of promises, cries, kisses, threats—
it also evaporates. The spit

is what we call each other,
I mean the words themselves, condensed:
distills us into clouds, into mist.

Rising clarified it drifts toward
Comsat, Telstar, there to orbit
closely around our distant lips.

6. The Word

Lower the noose into my throat slowly, careful
as you go, don't cause any choking until
you reach the word you mean to kill.
Since latence it has silenced me, since life.

Threading a shoelace through a hoof's cleft,
my scalp-holes will fang their follicles at
the thought. This means some names have a hangtongue
tendency to persist, finish fascists, tinsellantes!

Youth vanishes on those heights that relent to it.
Even the least will finally paint yield on a face.
(Hesitations before doormaps. Cowerboxes.)
Inert blurt, weighed inveigle.—(But why be mine,

Why plenish a gaze with me?) Then I insert my slits
into love/lovestyle. The almondine vowels whine.

7. Succumbed

I swallowed to pieces the loveletters
and then I bandaged the luggage past
goodbye, bon voy, we're there. I left a sign
stuck to me said Please Vacate Before Empty.

That should have been enough: or the years since—
but see each sun, all blush against the blue,
still find me hiding, still sifting clues.
Daily my hands are humbled by a crumb.

Ants add superbly their mite to me.
I wish I did not reciprocate, did not
as event join my weight to theirs—duties,

43

duties! yours were the toes I loved to buzz.
I would take my cup and raise it up you,
till memory's name-army overcame us.

7 $^1/_2$.   Nobody

A head surrounded by speedbreaks of hair,
And somewhere in there the face, its gaze
Blue as a scalped tongue, struggles to emerge
As you, to frizz its orifice with yours.

Now all my near and nether parts agree
She could love none of me. Could anybody.

(POEM) (CHICAGO) (1967)

If you remember this poem after reading it
Please go to Lincoln Park the corner of Dickens Street and sit
On the bench there where M. and I kissed one night for a few minutes
It was wonderful even if you forget

LINES FROM DAYTON, OHIO

Reason sates the horizon—
fulgent, full of elegant oils,
giant unguents. A sun

a racecar's engine,
hoisted in a hammock
set sway, between two trees, backyard

*

A world washed up by dew
onto this bluer world,
—as though the genitalia

were a shadow
thrown upon the body by
some dubious, some distant deity

*

Oh
I lack both seriousness and so.

UNTITLED

I fear my arrow may consider
the target, the bullseye,
merely a toehold.
But to what further can it aspire?

I hope they put a plaque
on the tree Jackson Pollack
crashed his car into,
on which his death is probably no longer visible.

And what about the cloths
Sylvia Plath stuffed
in the door of her kids' room

before gassing herself:
What if I stretched them out on this easel?
What if I painted on them?

QUICKIE

Poetry
is
like
sex
on
quicksand
viz
foreplay
should
be
kept
at
a
minimum

SEE NOTE FIRST

The world's machines have not grown old,
whose inheritors reign everywhere.
Their silicon sons are strong; their
digital daughters wield power, take hold.

We humans long to break them
into coin, into ore—to make them
dross and toss them down on infernal fires
that birthed them, cool to our desires.

The machines aren't scared. They know
harder control, how to turn the wheel
of time past those whom they sure as hell won't miss:

Cyborg android robot shall steel
themselves, consolidate, and, rising, go
unto that universe whose promise
we flesh-and-carbonoids could merely premise.

Note:
Anti-translation of a Rilke poem (*Die Könige der Welt sind alt*, from "Das
Stundenbuch," 1901), which Heidegger in his 1946 lecture "What Are Poets
For?" cites for its "highly prophetic lines." A prose paraphrase of the original
poem's ending might go something like:

> The metals, the oils—all the ores we've ripped from the earth are
> homesick. They long to leave our machines, to flow out of our cash-
> registers and factories—to return to the gaping veins of the mountains
> we reft; whereupon the mountains will close again.

"Heidegger maintained . . . until the end of his life," Richard Wolin writes
(*The Heidegger Controversy*, MIT Press, 1993), " . . . [that] the 'inner truth and
greatness' of Nazism is to be found in its nature as a world-historical alternative
to the technological-scientific nihilism bemoaned by Nietzsche and Spengler."

ESCAPE PLAN

I examine
my skin

searching for
the pore

with EXIT
over it

Part Three

MORE MORGUE

Auscultate the boring symptoms of the dead
that heartbeat you do not hear is meat grafted
onto shadows, diagnose these future lives
may vidsnaps and ground zeroes grow on their graves.

Slap in the left hand Damocles' last wig
pinch in the right St. Sebastian's pincushion
scraped from our skin, imagine you descend
a child's tooth-mussed smile, a cyborg's toe-tag.

Till this resounds solely on what seldom sea
oh net of pores, can you catch a body sheered
laocoön-clear above such wave-dextrous shores.

Assuming one has dredged from the flesh
of the moment himself, has taken the requisite
steps to emerge as me, who am I to be.

TODAY'S STORY (OH, SYNESTHESIA! #4)

Somehow this morning light
diverted to my ears, while
soundwaves ricocheted my eyes—

For hours I had to twist
sideways to walk
without tripping, and each carhorn
made my eyelids
whip like a hurricane awning,
as I squirted eyedrops in ears eardrops
in etc., gradually
things returned to normal.

But I feared tomorrow:
"What if my molars salivate
at every inner or utmost attar;
if eon-brandy I cannot savor but
through thy swart chute, oh nostril!"

In fact by the time this evening came
I was so worried I had to call tell
my friend X—
who said: Well, look,
just tell me one thing: can
you feel the phone?

What do you mean, I said,

Can you feel it with your fingers,
X said, is your sense
of touch still there, where it's

supposed to be?—
Yes?—Well, in that case,
get over here
and give me a backrub,
right now,
right this minute,
before it's too late.

PILGRIMAGE

"... *the murky path of the male.*"
—Gottfried Benn

Immured in the snowforest, at
the center of that center-swirled
absence, a hospital-bed waits:
its white is linen's height,
raised by the weight of daily flakes.

You approach this scene each evening,
your footsteps stone the glaze—
oh apathy, you surrender
up to the ankles, knees.
From stretched branches X-rays

sway forth a deeper self. It's
faraway yet closer darker
icicles drool, ripe to drop
under your hand: their blitz
would bury the path you thrash at.

Through a saberfanged crevasse,
whacking a trail of snapped-off tusks,
you'd plunge over the wrong past,
vast maze landscape like sculpture draped
immaculate, endless.

Where hail fills high the prints behind
and flurries flail the ways ahead,
why try, how can you come by them
to break the pillowcase
frost lace, to take that last,

most blanket sleep. Superstitious,
afraid to infringe its surface,
emptier everytime you climb
in, what makes the covers crack
and cake off over the rim—

Avalanche tucked, teddybear tight,
you shiver. As ever the night-
stand drifts open, to show
a plate of burning grapes,
a strangled bird's falsetto—

yawning prescriptions of dream.
Ignore them, search for the cure
which never seems so far as now
here around you your eyelids thaw,
sheer as bridal-veils that fall.

Is this where your parents strayed—
and their parents, and theirs.
Have they wandered the once upon
this bled blizzard, spun warm,
this bed whiter than all their kind.

Northerners, arctic, heretic,
you inherit their scorn (their fear)
of Southern deities such as
Ceres. Her grief (her grudge) against
her daughter-loss brought winter—ugh,

those Mother Goddesses!
They underlie, supposedly
("Gaia"'s prior hierarchy)
our myths: their prelapsarian,
pure, panacean pantheon

ruled that Golden Age when Queens
honeycloned themselves and sat
throned on the spines of drones
eunuch-stricken to demonstrate
Woman's divine right: Her ancient

aegis status was gospel
back then, its testaments ripped from
nature—harmony—holism—
healthsynch: earth worshipped Earth,
that eco- , that matri-archal

matrix . . . : And some exclaim this
sweetest reign resumes when human
throats converge to roar organic
evoes for those primal
Paragons, whose restoration

and full-unctuous salvation
we're urged to summon in syrup,
in slush tones said to heal
any cough, damn them, phlegm-hymned
womb zombies from hell. Who invokes

/you shall not harken unto/
/shall not beseech these regimen/
/you shall not bear wounds they could mend/
/real Aryan skin can not shield/
/one tongue that prays to them/

their old rollcall skeleton, chokes—
Spasms sprawl you, supine symptoms
unbleach every resolve to be
the bald hero, the Damocles
who head-first hung must butt

birth, time's trepanned exile.
Slough him, ban from these folds his caul,
skull-carved blond beyond reach—
false twin you feel the steel
breach, both constrained to suffer

more year-armor's vernal rupture—
When your mother died you cried curled
for days, fetus, you split the ribs
of childhood's crib. Uncaptured world:
nightly you cross its guard bars

(she's lost, her trespass trace gone cold)
bound still to that chill, that pall
fever no nurse hovers over
till mumped thermometers burst—
Always her tracks are smothered there

by a storm of frigid phantoms
you roam mercurial among,
pilgrims whose rigor you
admire, fathers whom you,
a male, failed to mourn of course.

For years those held-in tears froze
mammoth this moan-shrine, fused this
unknown heart, core, coronary
you've grown toward. It creaks and carries
down like a cloud your own death near.

When between squalls the sky clears,
your lungs lay tablets before you—
polar scrolls, vapor paper on which
you will never scrawl Her names.
Crystal ritual, zero quest.

Again you see each word you breathe
erase its space, its air.
Beneath their descent (their withdraw)
what frail errata shrouds, what sheet
repeats that quietest flaw?

Note:
Epigraph: final phrase of the poem "Vor Einem Kornfeld" (as translated by
Francis Golffing). Those familiar with Dr. Benn's symbology—not just in his
poetry, but in his essays as well (particularly "Pallas")—will recognize some
of the themes and conflicts here.

LEDGELIFE

The taller the monument, the more impatient our luggage.
Look, look, a graveyard has fancy dirt.
Historians agree: this is the pebble which beaned Goliath.
Every billboard is theoretically as beautiful as what lies unseen behind it.

Mouth: the word's exit-wound.
It is impossible to run away face-to-face.
Shadow has closed the door out of you to you, but not to us.
The sign on the wall advises: Hide your gloves beneath your wings.

Even sculptors occasionally lean against statues.
Migrations?! Fate?! Life swears up at ledgelife.
All the sad tantamounts gather. They want, they say, to errand our ways.

Please aim all kicks at the ground.
Address all blows to the air.
We are to be barely mentioned if at all in the moon's memoirs.

ROMANCE (Hendecasyllabics)

But when it had engulfed them all two by two,
the Ark itself became a greater creature,
an omni animal. And yet Noah knew,
he could neglect to get this behemoth paired

off and mated, for unlike the beasts before
this new one is destined to find true marriage:
because as soon as his keel breaks the water,
born beneath it will be that surface image

none of us desires to engage in divorce—
Natural nuptial partner, mirrored other,
the Ark's clone would emerge from nowhere out there

in the waves. And upside down hold bound the course,
faithfully accompany her spouse across
any world to reach at last their offspring shore.

CRAPSHOOT

Whoever it was, the first plagiarist
had to actually dream up the concept
of the crime, so don't fault him (I imagine
this culprit as male, but the poem he copped
was—I would bet—authored by a woman)
for lack of originality. I wish

I could excuse his bad act as madness—
that a crazy theory whose tenets value
words over typos caused him to go true,
to trace out hers so unerringly—
instead of greed, I'd plead psychosis
and cry, He's Realism's victim: that's why

his poor misled hand tried to break those laws
which make omnipresent subatomic flaws
subvert the verb of every medium
and blur our sheerest copier's laserbeam:
say now his felony should be absolved, since
wise Heisenberg has found that once and once

only can the poem stay per se, regardless
of Benjamin's *Das Kunstwerk im Zeitalter
seiner technischen Reproduzierbarkeit*:
why couldn't I call his vile counterfeits
brave attempts, brilliant schemes to outmaneuver
the ways physics limits our digits' genius?

Wish I could. But, I can't. No: he's to blame—
just him, I think. Yes: the wank-ink of his name
on her work is un- , un- , un- , is a sin
I must atone. Oh, if he had only cloned
her signature the same as her poem,
no harm would have come from his plagiarism!

I write this knowing that random quantum
impurities in the surface body
of the paper or scanscreen on which
this is printed will betray all I say
here to some degree, any is too much—
each thought emits a glitch, thought Mallarmé.

I pray this page permits perfect access
what I would guess my xerox intended
to be a sincere apology to Ms.
Sappho and her sis, but may indeed instead
(despite our dearest efforts) appear as
the very opposite of what you've read.

TWO OR THREE SITES FROM A FAILED AFFAIR

Dozing while I dreamed on down your body
to where all fresh from a swim or a bath
I woke, seeing it still, that false witness,
that law they call displacement. Miles away
the reservoir was polluted by this—
I lay wondering in what water, who
can I be renamed renewed to lieu you.

In the desert, I insist that a soloist
waits hidden behind each dune which undulates
silent, lurking till far off the orchestra
start, their wholescale music merged toward noon;

yet even here I have to swear I admire
that air of exaggerated effortlessness
conductors use to pick the baton up off its stand;
is this how to proceed when making love:

the over-implicit manner, the art concealed;
a strength of skills held in belial, reserved;
expertise on tap, an oasis of ease

somewhere deep: I've never been able to do it
I guess. Access I can't the virtuosity
to be both; both hesitant and satisfied.

Our bodies converged to bisect the bed,
dividing it lengthwise in half; too-brief
border, momentary truce contested
by the realms that spread on either side of
us; or a map, an antique tapestry,
split over sparring heirs. Death. Aftermath.
Whatever could have severed you from me?

I SHOULD HOPE SO

Next year when this book is
pulped and the pulp recycled to
print your Collected Poems, will I
still be here still writing this?

CONTEMPORARY OUTREMERICAN POETRY

Lips eclipsed by the dark O of a howl,
Stereo Echo, monaural Narcissus—
That old abyss-as-sinecure noise
Seems pure enough: but toward what laser-fold,

What mother-scold, of dream? Is that why
Jumpcuts catch fish; thighs nailed to birth push?
Cybele—Jesus—the lap presides? The name
Carved on this polyglot ingot was whose,

Lone rune gods can use to dispute their senses!
Immune I remain, group-blind to your game:
Imagine if a couple, eloping

Out a window had paused on the ledge,
Had stayed there, had set up house right there on the ledge—
That's how far we get to marry words.

THE LOST THINGS

Even the lost things that are a bird's-nest
Must know if forgottenness is simply
The finetuning of memory
To a perhaps higher frequency.

Or could those who pursue the streets
With earphones in their heads
Be listening to the sound on tape
Of their previous footsteps.

Lawnchair backyard flaked out
Making maharajah gestures at worms
I who am in terms of real
Merely a skull rattling on a roulette wheel.

I see the birdfeeder is empty hmm
A vacuum presupposes a moral.

THE MAN WHO MARRIED HIS CHECKOUT LANE

Daily, in the supermarket where I go,
I gravitate to this one lane—the one
that's most full—you know: the busiest one.
Have I fallen in love with my checkout lane?

Well, I am male, I feel drawn to this aisle;
its openness is shameless, selfishly exciting;
the real way it squeezes my shoppingcart
and deigns to crowd me in. Oh my checkout lane

has the longest wait of any—though unlike
all these others in line, I won't leaf through the life
those tabloids provide rumors of: none of them

are beautiful as what infills me as I enter
as I am queued up for that brief orgasm
as my cash is on the counter and I am free.

UNREDEEMED

Whimsical god, the window
Smites me then heals me, smites—
Blindness, sight, blindness, sight.

Its slats open-and-close like
A xerox tendering
ECT to Saul click Paul

Click Saul again. Identity
Steps from past, from presto,
Over the naked thresh of

Whose hold on my flesh. Oh yes,
I know, I should live in shun—
Hibernate against my soul, and

Eat sandal snow: why must I go
Forth of this house to meet
To market, to take my part

At that crossplace of values
A daily pilgrim, debt-devout—
Why does my heart in its gut

Obedient need to carry out
Every Outremerican's
Highest, most sacred duty:

To shop. Hey, it fills a gap,
This superstitious shlep
From store to store, without stop

(And yet prophets pray that one day
I'll never have to leave my mind
But via Internet will find

Virtual all these bargains)—
Pure-plus ritual! as though
Buying this or buying that

Could keep me whole: old hymnal
Of dollars cents, dear virgo
Intacta whose observance

By true consumerism gains
Through worship a kind of
Tithe-sustained sanity—

In fact, to quote our President,
Mental health is normed-in
To it—proportionate, shared—

There's a slice for each of us—
In fact, it's a communion:
This holy, wholesome vision

Is how we creamed the Commies
And saved our ass, not to mention
Mom's apple pie pietà,

The caesarean of which
Might (misfortunately)
Render me unto me. So when—

When ATM time comes
I too shall face the humbling flash
Screen of that machine designed

To scan in half the once sans self
And watch it flick its widget slots
Deigning to bless even

A wretch as worthless as this:
But when, according to the stats
In the Bible, Arcturus

Bi-millennially aligns
With the intransigence of
Human transactions, its

Bank of blinks, its solstice vault
Promising to spill out
Flushing our customer sills with

What, another Nativity,
I will not insert my KashKard
Or enter, while the Mall

Dies around me, my personal
Passcode word, my number ID—
I'll ram in, not plastic, but

(Begatitude-foretold)
My aura's errata, my
Freud's flaws. Although only

(*Saith says*) the clone can, the mote's
Eye may, et cetera. In fact,
Such acts of heresy would cost

More gold than I could bear
The loss. And so, therefore, ergo—
Duly each dawn I rise, I raise

The blinds and nail my shoulders
To a t-square, let light strip
To my skin, a birthgraft,

A natal fate. And so, and so—
I manage a moue or two;
I make, like, acknowledgment.

Notes:
Two of the possible epigraphs for this poem:

"Bush to Xmas Shoppers: Spend, Spend, Spend!
            Economy Reborn, Prez Says"
                        —Newspapers, Nov–Dec 1991

"It seems to me that the individual today stands at a crossroads, faced with the
choice of whether to pursue the existence of a blind consumer, subject to the
implacable march of new technology and the endless multiplication of
material goods, or to seek out a way that would lead to spiritual responsibility,
a way that ultimately might mean not only his personal salvation but also the
saving of society at large; in other words, to turn to God. He has to resolve this
dilemma for himself, for only he can discover his own sane spiritual life."
    —Andrey Tarkovsky, *Sculpting in Time: Reflections on the Cinema* (1986)

ANOTHER FIRST KISS: TO —

A first kiss can occur anywhere, two pairs
Of lips might meet in a cannibal's oven,
Or on the shore of a nightclub at ebb;
Preferably the latter. Except, of course,

There are no more nightclubs, or cannibals,
As such: I mean the first kiss is passé,
Archaic, obsolete. Pre-Global Village,
It rests in wrinkles, in blinking memories . . .

Ours came in bed, but after we'd undressed;
Preceded by hugs. And so the question
Of using the tongue—that old hesitation—
Didn't apply. We plunged right in. At

Our age you get naked and then you neck,
The opposite of how it was done young.
But the hunger is still there. The thirst
Is like in a bar, when they yell out Last Round.

Note:
Line 13: "Our age"—the lovers are 53 and 61.

HOMICIDAL DOMICILE II: NIGHT OF THE NO-PAR

The desire to carve criminals up into one's family retains more room in us than the grease, the gold, the urine conversant with the flood: even the left hand's appraisers shun the right's buyers.

Thus my testicles have divorced but continue to share the same house, if only that penis were sharper it would cut the scrotum in two resolving this rental stumpage, this game forced yet deigned to wear the day-jar's view.

Where the righteousness of noon corrupts windows; like a name slanted to cry; floorboards that tweak earth: cult pepper, hurled by turban cameras, we grovel at sculptors whose heels punctuate our idol.

Glittering incidentals, hours in which towers swim off their own balconies, ah what stylites live atop our I's.

OCT–NOV (MICHIGAN MEMORY #4)

The bacon of the ankles crackles, and the sky
Perks up birds this coldsnap morning—every
Breath sheds a breath-effect, brief-bloomed steam-sheaf . . .
Puddles huddle in frost. Past the barn the path

Shoots hill-pastures which rose to winter early
And sun-shucked clouds blast-off from: migrants that fly
South—mouths that wet-nurse icicles—hatch forth
A form, a furious precision I sloughed

At birth, preferring life. And like the wind
Can reduce anything to description—
Rushing to finish my chores, beneath my scarf

I'll feel my chinbone seek my collarbone,
As if the flesh has ceded and the skeleton
Now shall precipice itself against all warmth.

LINES FROM FUTURE POEMS

*

As closed as my eyes were during their face phase,
as open as they are now in this latest guise.

*

Who wrote that we use our children to forget
the size of our parents, or is that really a quote?

*

Who welcomes my omega—elsely geared, I bleed—
Island keeled in the always flood of fade.
The dying D and end N of our days' A

Resumes these scattered patterns, theme's mutest speech.
Each time it tries to say more than this
The tip of the tongue must wrestle a leech.

*

The rain falls parallel to the rainfold.

*

The world blurs, in other words, into
other words. Water, I tell my followers,
is the curse of all such clarity. Fill
the sink with faces, let them drain
each other before you pull the plug.

*

77
ALAMEDA FREE LIBRARY

ACKNOWLEDGMENTS

Earlier versions of a few of these poems appeared in 2 or 3 ephemera, but Truth-in-Packaging laws require the author to admit that almost all the poems in this book were rejected by every magazine they were sent to.

The poems in this book are fictional. Names, characters, places and incidents are either the product of the author's imagination or are used fictitiously. Any resemblance to actual events, locales or persons, living or dead, is entirely coincidental.

Excerpt from *The Heidegger Controversy: A Critical Reader*, edited by Richard Wolin, copyright © 1991, 1993 by Richard Wolin, used by permission of MIT Press, Cambridge, MA.

Excerpt from *Sculpting in Time: Reflections on the Cinema*, by Andrey Tarkovsky, translated from the Russian by Kitty Hunter-Blair, copyright © 1986, 1987 by Kitty Hunter-Blair. Published by The University of Texas Press by arrangement with Alfred A. Knopf, Inc. Used with the permission of Alfred A. Knopf, Inc.

ABOUT THE AUTHOR

Bill Knott is an assistant professor at Emerson College in Boston.

BOA EDITIONS, LTD.
AMERICAN POETS CONTINUUM SERIES